D0049114

Presented to:

_____

From:

_____

Date:

_____

Jesus Calling®
FOR
Christmas

Sarah Young

Thomas Nelson
Since 1798

Published in Nashville, Tennessee, by Thomas Nelson. Thomas Nelson is a registered trademark of HarperCollins Christian Publishing, Inc.

Unless otherwise noted, Scripture quotations are taken from the Holy Bible, New International Version®, NIV®. Copyright © 1973, 1978, 1984 by Biblica, Inc.® Used by permission of Zondervan. All rights reserved worldwide. www.zondervan.com. The "NIV" and "New International Version" are trademarks registered in the United States Patent and Trademark Office by Biblica, Inc.®

Scripture quotations marked AMP are from the Amplified® Bible. Copyright © 1954, 1958, 1962, 1964, 1965, 1987 by The Lockman Foundation. Used by permission. (www.Lockman.org) Scripture quotations marked ESV are from the ESV® Bible (The Holy Bible, English Standard Version®), copyright © 2001 by Crossway, a publishing ministry of Good News Publishers. Used by permission. All rights reserved. Scripture quotations marked NASB are from New American Standard Bible®. Copyright © 1960, 1962, 1963, 1968, 1971, 1972, 1973, 1975, 1977, 1995 by The Lockman Foundation. Used by permission. (www.Lockman.org) Scripture quotations marked NKJV are from the New King James Version®. © 1982 by Thomas Nelson. Used by permission. All rights reserved. Scripture quotations marked NLT are from the Holy Bible, New Living Translation. © 1996, 2004, 2007, 2013, 2015 by Tyndale House Foundation. Used by permission of Tyndale House Publishers, Inc., Carol Stream, Illinois 60188. All rights reserved.

Devotions are excerpted from *Jesus Calling*®, *Jesus Today*®, and *Jesus Always*.

ISBN 978-1-4003-0918-4
ISBN 978-1-4041-1213-1 (custom)
ISBN 978-1-4041-1208-7 (custom)

Printed in China

20 21 22 23 24 DSC 7 6

Dear Reader,

May the pages of this book help you enjoy both the beauty of God's glorious creation and the wonder of His priceless gift to us—His only Son, Jesus, born in a humble stable. As we celebrate the birth of Jesus, let us remember that He came into the world to provide eternal life for all who believe in Him.

These devotions are written from the perspective of Jesus speaking to you, the reader. I have included Scripture with each devotion, and I encourage you to read both—slowly and thoughtfully.

I will be praying for readers of *Jesus Calling for Christmas*. Remember that Jesus is Immanuel, God with us. May you enjoy His Presence and His Peace in ever-increasing measure.

Merry Christmas!
Sarah Young

For to us a *child* is born, to us a *son* is given. . . .
And he will be called Wonderful Counselor,
Mighty God, Everlasting Father, Prince of *Peace*.

—ISAIAH 9:6

When I entered your world as the God-Man, *I came to that which was My own.* Everything belongs to Me! Most people think their possessions are their own, but the truth is, you—and everything you possess—belong to Me. Though you may feel isolated and alone at times, this is only an illusion. I bought you at an astronomical price, so you are Mine—My treasure. The colossal price I paid shows how precious you are to Me! Ponder this powerful truth whenever you start to doubt your worth. You are My cherished one, *saved by grace through faith* in Me, your Savior.

Because you are precious to Me, I want you to take good care of yourself: spiritually, emotionally, and physically. Make time for pondering Scripture in your mind and heart. Protect yourself, both emotionally and physically, from those who would take advantage of you. Remember that *your body is the Holy Spirit's temple.* I also want you to help others discover the glorious good news—the free gift of *eternal Life for all who believe in Me.*.

He came to that which was his own, but
his own did not receive him.

JOHN 1:11

For it is by grace you have been saved, through
faith—and this not from yourselves, it is the gift of
God—not by works, so that no one can boast.

EPHESIANS 2:8—9

Do you not know that your body is a temple of the
Holy Spirit, who is in you, whom you have received
from God? You are not your own; you were bought
at a price. Therefore honor God with your body.

1 CORINTHIANS 6:19—20

"For *God* so *loved* the world that he gave his one and only Son, that whoever *believes* in him shall not perish but have *eternal* life."

JOHN 3:16

When an angel announced My birth to *shepherds living out in the fields near Bethlehem*, he told them: *Do not be afraid. I bring you good news of great Joy.* The instruction to not be afraid is repeated in the Bible more than any other command. It is a tender, merciful directive—and it is for you! I know how prone to fear you are, and I do not condemn you for it. However, I *do* want to help you break free from this tendency.

Joy is a powerful antidote to fear! And the greater the Joy, the more effective an antidote it is. The angel's announcement to the shepherds was one of *great* Joy. Don't ever lose sight of what amazingly *good news* the gospel is! You repent of your sins and trust Me as Savior. I forgive *all* your sins, changing your ultimate destination from hell to heaven. Moreover, I give you *Myself*—lavishing My Love upon you, promising you My Presence forever. Take time to ponder the angel's glorious proclamation to the shepherds. *Rejoice in Me*, beloved.

And there were shepherds living out in the fields nearby,
keeping watch over their flocks at night. An angel of
the Lord appeared to them, and the glory of the Lord
shone around them, and they were terrified. But the
angel said to them, "Do not be afraid. I bring you good
news of great joy that will be for all the people."

LUKE 2:8–10

How great is the love the Father has lavished
on us, that we should be called children of God!
And that is what we are! The reason the world
does not know us is that it did not know him.

1 JOHN 3:1

Rejoice in the Lord always. Again I will say, rejoice!

PHILIPPIANS 4:4 NKJV

I am the greatest Gift imaginable! When you have *Me*, you have everything you need—for this life and the next. I have promised *to meet all your needs according to My glorious riches*. Yet My loved ones sometimes fail to enjoy the riches I provide because of an ungrateful attitude. Instead of rejoicing in all that they have, they long for what they do not have. As a result, they become discontented.

I'm training you to practice *the sacrifice of thanksgiving—* thanking Me *in all circumstances*. First, give thanks for the blessings you can see in your life. Then stop and ponder the awesome gift of knowing Me. I am your living God, your loving Savior, your constant Companion. No matter how much or how little you have in this world, your relationship with Me makes you immeasurably rich. So whenever you are counting your blessings, be sure to include the infinite wealth you have in Me. Add Me into the equation, and your gratitude will grow exponentially. Whatever you have + Me = an incalculable fortune!

And my God will meet all your needs according
to his glorious riches in Christ Jesus.

PHILIPPIANS 4:19

I will offer to You the sacrifice of thanksgiving,
and will call upon the name of the LORD.

PSALM 116:17 NKJV

Give thanks in all circumstances, for this
is God's will for you in Christ Jesus.

1 THESSALONIANS 5:18

$\mathcal{I}$ am the *Prince of Peace*. As I said to My disciples, I say also to you: *Peace be with you*. Since I am your constant Companion, My Peace is steadfastly with you. When you keep your focus on Me, you experience both My Presence and My Peace. Worship Me as King of kings, Lord of lords, and Prince of Peace.

You need My Peace each moment to accomplish My purposes in your life. Sometimes you are tempted to take shortcuts in order to reach your goal as quickly as possible. But if the shortcut requires turning your back on My peaceful Presence, you must choose the longer route. Walk with Me along paths of Peace; enjoy the journey in My Presence.

For to us a child is born, to us a son is given, and
the government will be on his shoulders. And
he will be called Wonderful Counselor, Mighty
God, Everlasting Father, Prince of Peace.

ISAIAH 9:6

On the evening of that first day of the week, when the
disciples were together, with the doors locked for fear
of the Jews, Jesus came and stood among them and said,
"Peace be with you!" After he said this, he showed them
his hands and side. The disciples were overjoyed when
they saw the Lord. Again Jesus said, "Peace be with
you! As the Father has sent me, I am sending you."

JOHN 20:19–21

Show me Your ways, O LORD; teach me Your paths.

PSALM 25:4 NKJV

*A*s you wait attentively in My Presence, *the Light of the knowledge of My Glory* shines upon you. This radiant knowledge transcends all understanding. It transforms every fiber of your being: renewing your mind, cleansing your heart, invigorating your body. Open yourself fully to My Presence; be awed by My glorious Being.

Try to imagine what I gave up when I came into your world as a baby. I set aside My Glory so that I could identify with mankind. I accepted the limitations of infancy under the most appalling conditions—a filthy stable. There was nothing glorious about that setting, though angels lit up the sky proclaiming, "Glory!" to awestruck shepherds.

When you sit quietly with Me, the process I went through is reversed in your experience. As you identify with Me, heaven's vistas open up before you—granting you glimpses of My Glory. *I became poor so that you might become rich.* Sing hallelujahs to My holy Name!

For God, who said, "Let light shine out of darkness," made his light shine in our hearts to give us the light of the knowledge of the glory of God in the face of Christ.

2 CORINTHIANS 4:6

Who, being in very nature God, did not consider equality with God something to be grasped, but made himself nothing, taking the very nature of a servant, being made in human likeness.

PHILIPPIANS 2:6–7

Suddenly a great company of the heavenly host appeared with the angel, praising God and saying, "Glory to God in the highest."

LUKE 2:13–14

For you know the *grace* of our Lord *Jesus* Christ, that though he was rich, yet for your sakes he became *poor*, so that you through his poverty might become *rich*.

2 CORINTHIANS 8:9

*N*ever take for granted My intimate nearness. Marvel at the wonder of My continual Presence with you. Even the most ardent human lover cannot be with you always. Nor can another person know the intimacies of your heart, mind, and spirit. *I know everything about you—even the number of hairs on your head.* You don't need to work at revealing yourself to Me.

Many people spend a lifetime or a small fortune searching for someone who understands them. Yet I am freely available to all who call upon My Name, who open their hearts to receive Me as Savior. This simple act of faith is the beginning of a lifelong love story. I, the Lover of your soul, understand you perfectly and love you eternally.

The LORD is near to all who call upon Him,

to all who call upon Him in truth.

PSALM 145:18 NKJV

⟲

"Indeed, the very hairs of your head are all numbered.

Don't be afraid; you are worth more than many sparrows."

LUKE 12:7

⟲

Yet to all who received him, to those who believed in his

name, he gave the right to become children of God.

JOHN 1:12

Everyone who calls on the name
of the *Lord* will be *saved*.

ROMANS 10:13

Rest in Me, My child, forgetting about the worries of the world. Focus on Me—Immanuel—and let My living Presence envelop you in Peace. Tune in to My eternal security, for *I am the same yesterday, today, and forever.* If you live on the surface of life by focusing on ever-changing phenomena, you will find yourself echoing the words of Solomon: *"Meaningless! Meaningless! Everything is meaningless!"*

Living in collaboration with Me is the way to instill meaning into your days. Begin each day alone with Me so that you can experience the reality of My Presence. As you spend time with Me, the way before you opens up step by step. Arise from the stillness of our communion, and gradually begin your journey through the day. Hold My hand in deliberate dependence on Me, and I will smooth out the path before you.

All this took place to fulfill what the Lord had
said through the prophet: "The virgin will be with
child and will give birth to a son, and they will call
him Immanuel"—which means, "God with us."

MATTHEW 1:22–23

Jesus Christ is the same yesterday and today and forever.

HEBREWS 13:8

"Meaningless! Meaningless!" says the Teacher.
"Utterly meaningless! Everything is meaningless."

ECCLESIASTES 1:2

In all your ways acknowledge him, and
he will make your paths straight.

PROVERBS 3:6

*D*o not be weighed down by the clutter in your life: lots of little chores to do sometime, in no particular order. If you focus too much on these petty tasks, trying to get them all out of the way, you will discover that they are endless. They can eat up as much time as you devote to them.

Instead of trying to do all your chores at once, choose the ones that need to be done today. Let the rest slip into the background of your mind so I can be in the forefront of your awareness. Remember that your ultimate goal is living close to Me, being responsive to My initiatives. I can communicate with you most readily when your mind is uncluttered and turned toward Me. Seek My Face continually throughout this day. Let My Presence bring order to your thoughts, infusing Peace into your entire being.

Commit to the LORD whatever you do,
and your plans will succeed.

PROVERBS 16:3

❧

"But seek first his kingdom and his righteousness,
and all these things will be given to you as well."

MATTHEW 6:33

❧

When You said, "Seek My face," my heart said
to You, "Your face, LORD, I will seek."

PSALM 27:8 NKJV

❧

You will keep him in perfect peace, whose mind
is stayed on You, because he trusts in You.

ISAIAH 26:3 NKJV

I am with you in all that you do, even in the most menial task. I am always aware of you, concerned with every detail of your life. Nothing escapes My notice—not even *the number of hairs on your head*. However, your awareness of My Presence falters and flickers; as a result, your life experience feels fragmented. When your focus is broad enough to include Me in your thoughts, you feel safe and complete. When your perception narrows so that problems or details fill your consciousness, you feel empty and incomplete.

Learn to look steadily at Me in all your moments and all your circumstances. Though the world is unstable and in flux, you can experience continuity through your uninterrupted awareness of My Presence. *Fix your gaze on what is unseen*, even as the visible world parades before your eyes.

"Are not two sparrows sold for a penny? Yet not one of them will fall to the ground apart from the will of your Father. And even the very hairs of your head are all numbered. So don't be afraid; you are worth more than many sparrows."

MATTHEW 10:29–31

By faith he left Egypt, not fearing the king's anger; he persevered because he saw him who is invisible.

HEBREWS 11:27

So we fix our eyes not on what is seen, but on what is unseen. For what is seen is temporary, but what is unseen is eternal.

2 CORINTHIANS 4:18

When I joined the ranks of humanity, born into the humblest conditions, My Glory was hidden from all but a few people. Occasionally, streaks of Glory shone out of Me, especially when I began to do miracles. Toward the end of My life, I was taunted and tempted to display more of My awesome Power than My Father's plan permitted. I could have called down legions of angels to rescue Me at any point. Imagine the self-control required of a martyr who could free Himself at will! All of this was necessary to provide the relationship with Me that you now enjoy. Let your life become a praise song to Me by proclaiming My glorious Presence in the world.

This, the first of his miraculous signs, Jesus performed at Cana in Galilee. He thus revealed his glory, and his disciples put their faith in him.

JOHN 2:11

The people stood watching, and the rulers even sneered at him. They said, "He saved others; let him save himself if he is the Christ of God, the Chosen One." The soldiers also came up and mocked him. They offered him wine vinegar.

LUKE 23:35–36

It is good to praise the LORD and make music to your name, O Most High, to proclaim your love in the morning and your faithfulness at night, to the music of the ten-stringed lyre and the melody of the harp. For you make me glad by your deeds, O LORD; I sing for joy at the works of your hands. How great are your works, O LORD, how profound your thoughts!

PSALM 92:1–5

I am *the Rock that is higher than you* and your circumstances. I am *your* Rock in whom you can take refuge—any time, any place. Come to Me, beloved; rest in the Peace of My Presence. Take a break from trying to figure everything out. Admit that many, many things are beyond your understanding—and your control. *My ways and thoughts are higher than yours, as the heavens are higher than the earth.*

When the world around you looks confusing and evil appears to be winning, remember this: I am the Light that keeps on shining in all situations. And light *always* overcomes darkness whenever these two opposites meet face to face.

Since you are My follower, I want you to shine brightly in this troubled world. Whisper My Name; sing songs of praise. Tell others *good tidings of great Joy*—that I am the *Savior, who is Christ the Lord*! I am also the One who is with you continually. Keep looking to Me, and My Presence will illuminate your path.

From the ends of the earth I call to you, I call as my heart
grows faint; lead me to the rock that is higher than I.

PSALM 61:2

The LORD is my rock, my fortress and my deliverer;
my God is my rock, in whom I take refuge. He is my
shield and the horn of my salvation, my stronghold.

PSALM 18:2

"As the heavens are higher than the earth,
so are my ways higher than your ways and
my thoughts than your thoughts."

ISAIAH 55:9

Then the *angel* said to them, "Do not be afraid, for behold, I bring you good tidings of great joy which will be to all people. For there is *born* to you this day in the city of David a *Savior*, who is Christ the Lord."

LUKE 2:10–11 NKJV

*J*n Isaiah's prophecy about My birth, he referred to Me as *Eternal Father*. There is unity of essence in the Trinity, even though it is comprised of three Persons. When the Jews were questioning Me in the temple, I went so far as to say: *"I and the Father are one."* Later, when Philip asked Me to show the Father to the disciples, I said: *"Anyone who has seen Me has seen the Father."* So never think of Me as just a great teacher. I am God, and the Father and I live in perfect unity.

As you come to know Me in greater depth and breadth, realize that you are also growing closer to the Father. Don't let the mysterious richness of the Trinity confuse you. Simply come to Me, recognizing that I am everything you could ever need Me to be. I—your only Savior—am sufficient for you.

In the midst of this busy Advent season, keep bringing your focus back to My holy Presence. Remember that *Immanuel* has come, and rejoice!

For a child will be born to us, a son will be given to us; and the government will rest on His shoulders; and His name will be called Wonderful Counselor, Mighty God, Eternal Father, Prince of Peace.

ISAIAH 9:6 NASB

"I and the Father are one."

JOHN 10:30

Jesus answered: "Don't you know me, Philip, even after I have been among you such a long time? Anyone who has seen me has seen the Father. How can you say, 'Show us the Father'?"

JOHN 14:9

"Behold, the virgin shall be with *child*, and bear a Son, and they shall call His name *Immanuel*," which is translated, "God with us."

MATTHEW 1:23 NKJV

hose who wait upon Me will gain new strength. Spending time alone with Me is so good for you, but it is increasingly countercultural. Multitasking and staying busy have become the norm. During the Advent season, there are even *more* things to be done and places to go. So I encourage you to break free from all the activity and demands for a while. *Seek My Face* and enjoy My Presence, remembering that Christmas is all about *Me*.

Waiting upon Me is an act of faith—trusting that prayer really does make a difference. *Come to Me with your weariness and burdens*, being candid and real with Me. Rest in My Presence, and tell Me about your concerns. Let Me lift the burdens from your aching shoulders. Trust that *I am able to do exceedingly abundantly above all you ask or think*.

As you arise from these quiet moments, hear Me whispering "I am with you" throughout the day. Rejoice in the *new strength* you have gained through spending time with Me.

Yet those who wait for the LORD will gain
new strength; they will mount up with wings
like eagles, they will run and not get tired,
they will walk and not become weary.

ISAIAH 40:31 NASB

When You said, "Seek My face," my heart said
to You, "Your face, LORD, I will seek."

PSALM 27:8 NKJV

"Come to me, all you who are weary and
burdened, and I will give you rest."

MATTHEW 11:28

Now to *Him* who is able
to do exceedingly abundantly
above all that we ask or
think, according to the
power that works in us.

Ephesians 3:20 nkjv

ing for Joy to Me, your Strength. Christmas music is one of the best blessings of the season, and it doesn't have to cost you anything. You can sing the carols at church or in the privacy of your home—or even in your car. As you are making a joyful noise, pay close attention to the words. They are all about Me and My miraculous entrance into your world through the virgin birth. Singing from your heart increases both your Joy and your energy. It also blesses Me.

I created you to glorify Me and enjoy Me forever. So it's not surprising that you feel more fully alive when you glorify Me through song. I want you to learn to enjoy Me in more and more aspects of your life. Before you arise from your bed each morning, try to become aware of My Presence with you. Say to yourself: *"Surely the Lord is in this place."* This will awaken your awareness to the wonders of My continual nearness. *I will fill you with Joy in My Presence.*

Sing for joy to God our strength; shout
aloud to the God of Jacob!

PSALM 81:1

But let all who take refuge in you rejoice; let them sing
joyful praises forever. Spread your protection over them,
that all who love your name may be filled with joy.

PSALM 5:11 NLT

When Jacob awoke from his sleep, he thought, "Surely
the LORD is in this place, and I was not aware of it."

GENESIS 28:16

You have made known
to me the *paths* of life;
you will fill me with
joy in your *presence*.

ACTS 2:28

I am *Immanuel—God with you* at all times. This promise provides a solid foundation for your Joy. Many people try to pin their pleasure to temporary things, but My Presence with you is eternal. Rejoice greatly, beloved, knowing that your Savior *will never leave you or forsake you.*

The nature of time can make it difficult for you to enjoy your life. On rare days when everything is going well, your awareness that the ideal conditions are fleeting can dampen your enjoyment of them. Even the most delightful vacation must eventually come to an end. Seasons of life also come and go, despite your longing at times to "stop the clock" and keep things just as they are.

Do not look down on temporary pleasures, but *do* recognize their limitations—their inability to quench the thirst of your soul. Your search for lasting Joy will fail unless you make *Me* the ultimate goal of your quest. *I will show you the way of Life. In My Presence is fullness of Joy.*

"The virgin will be with child and will give birth to a son, and they will call him Immanuel"—which means, "God with us."

MATTHEW 1:23

The LORD himself goes before you and will be with you; he will never leave you nor forsake you. Do not be afraid; do not be discouraged.

DEUTERONOMY 31:8

You will show me the path of life; in Your presence is fullness of joy; at Your right hand are pleasures forevermore.

PSALM 16:11 NKJV

I am your best Friend, as well as your King. Walk hand in hand with Me through your life. Together we will face whatever each day brings: pleasures, hardships, adventures, disappointments. Nothing is wasted when it is shared with Me. *I can bring beauty out of the ashes of lost dreams.* I can glean Joy out of sorrow, Peace out of adversity. Only a Friend who is also the King of kings could accomplish this divine alchemy. There is no other like Me!

The friendship I offer you is practical and down-to-earth, yet it is saturated with heavenly Glory. Living in My Presence means living in two realms simultaneously: the visible world and unseen, eternal reality. I have equipped you to stay conscious of Me while walking along dusty, earthbound paths.

"Greater love has no one than this, that he lay down his life for his friends. You are my friends if you do what I command. I no longer call you servants, because a servant does not know his master's business. Instead, I have called you friends, for everything that I learned from my Father I have made known to you."

JOHN 15:13–15

And provide for those who grieve in Zion—to bestow on them a crown of beauty instead of ashes, the oil of gladness instead of mourning, and a garment of praise instead of a spirit of despair. They will be called oaks of righteousness, a planting of the LORD for the display of his splendor.

ISAIAH 61:3

Sorrowful, yet always rejoicing; poor, yet making many rich; having nothing, and yet possessing everything.

2 CORINTHIANS 6:10

I became poor so that you might become rich. My incarnation—the essence of Christmas—was a gift of infinitely great value. However, it impoverished Me immeasurably! I gave up the majestic splendors of heaven to become a helpless baby. My parents were poor, young, and far away from home when I was born in a stable in Bethlehem.

I performed many miracles during My lifetime, but they were for the benefit of others, not Myself. After fasting forty days and nights in the wilderness, I was tempted by the devil to *turn stones into bread.* But I refused to do this miracle, even though I was so hungry. I lived as a homeless man for years.

Because I was willing to experience a life of poverty, you are incredibly rich! My life, death, and resurrection opened the way for My followers to become *children of God* and heirs of glorious, eternal riches. My abiding Presence is also a precious gift. Celebrate all these amazing gifts with gratitude and overflowing Joy!

For you know the grace of our Lord Jesus Christ, that
though he was rich, yet for your sakes he became poor,
so that you through his poverty might become rich.

2 CORINTHIANS 8:9

Jesus was led up by the Spirit into the wilderness to be
tempted by the devil. And when He had fasted forty days
and forty nights, afterward He was hungry. Now when the
tempter came to Him, he said, "If You are the Son of God,
command that these stones become bread." But He answered
and said, "It is written, 'Man shall not live by bread alone,
but by every word that proceeds from the mouth of God.'"

MATTHEW 4:1–4 NKJV

And the angel said to them, "Fear not, for behold, I bring
you good news of great joy that will be for all the people."

LUKE 2:10 ESV

To all who received him,
to those who *believed* in
his name, he gave the right to
become *children* of God.

John 1:12

I am the Light of the world! Many people celebrate Advent season by illuminating their homes with candles and decorated trees. This is a way of symbolizing My coming into the world—eternal Light breaking through the darkness and opening up the way to heaven. Nothing can reverse this glorious plan of salvation. All who trust Me as Savior are adopted into My royal family forever!

My Light shines on in the darkness, for the darkness has never overpowered it. No matter how much evil and unbelief you see in this dark world, I continue to shine brightly—a beacon of hope to those who have eyes that really see. So it's crucial to look toward the Light as much as possible. *Fix your eyes on Me*, beloved! Through thousands of good thought-choices, you can find Me—"see" Me—as you journey through this life. My Spirit can help you persevere in the delightful discipline of keeping your eyes on Me. *Whoever follows Me will never walk in darkness but will have the Light of Life.*

When Jesus spoke again to the people, he said, "I am the light of the world. Whoever follows me will never walk in darkness, but will have the light of life."

JOHN 8:12

God decided in advance to adopt us into his own family by bringing us to himself through Jesus Christ. This is what he wanted to do, and it gave him great pleasure.

EPHESIANS 1:5 NLT

And the Light shines on in the darkness, for the darkness has never overpowered it [put it out or absorbed it or appropriated it, and is unreceptive to it].

JOHN 1:5 AMP

Let us fix our eyes on Jesus, the author and perfecter of our *faith*, who for the joy set before him endured the *cross*, scorning its shame, and sat down at the right hand of the *throne* of God.

Hebrews 12:2

I am King of kings and Lord of lords, dwelling in dazzlingly bright Light! I am also your Shepherd, Companion, and Friend—the One who never lets go of your hand. Worship Me in My holy Majesty; come close to Me, and rest in My Presence. You need Me both as God and as Man. Only My Incarnation on that first, long-ago Christmas could fulfill your neediness. Since I went to such extreme measures to save you from your sins, you can be assured that I will *graciously give you all you need.*

Nurture well your trust in Me as Savior, Lord, and Friend. I have held back nothing in My provision for you. I have even deigned to live within you! Rejoice in all that I have done for you, and My Light will shine through you into the world.

Which God will bring about in his own time—God, the blessed and only Ruler, the King of kings and Lord of lords, who alone is immortal and who lives in unapproachable light, whom no one has seen or can see. To him be honor and might forever. Amen.

1 TIMOTHY 6:15–16

Come, let us bow down in worship, let us kneel before the LORD our Maker; for he is our God and we are the people of his pasture, the flock under his care.

PSALM 95:6–7

He who did not spare his own Son, but gave him up for us all—how will he not also, along with him, graciously give us all things?

ROMANS 8:32

And we have the *word* of the *prophets* made more certain, and you will do well to pay attention to it, as to a light *shining* in a dark place, until the day dawns and the morning *star* rises in your *hearts*.

2 PETER 1:19

*P*repare your heart for the celebration of My birth. Listen to the voice of John the Baptist: *"Prepare the way for the Lord; make straight paths for Him."*

Christmas is the time to exult in My miraculous incarnation, when *the Word became flesh and dwelt among you.* I identified with mankind to the ultimate extent—becoming a Man and taking up residence in your world. Don't let the familiarity of this astonishing miracle dull its effect on you. Recognize that I am the Gift above all gifts, and *rejoice in Me!*

Clear out clutter and open up your heart by pondering the wonders of My entrance into human history. View these events from the perspective of the shepherds, who were keeping watch over their flocks at night. They witnessed first one angel and then *a multitude* of them lighting up the sky, proclaiming: *"Glory to God in the highest, and on earth Peace among those with whom He is pleased!"* Gaze at the Glory of my birth, just as the shepherds did, and respond with childlike wonder.

"Prepare the way for the Lord, make
straight paths for him."

MARK 1:3

And the Word became flesh and dwelt among us,
and we have seen his glory, glory as of the only
Son from the Father, full of grace and truth.

JOHN 1:14 ESV

Rejoice in the Lord always. Again I will say, rejoice!

PHILIPPIANS 4:4 NKJV

And suddenly there was with the *angel* a multitude of the heavenly *host* praising God and saying, "Glory to God in the highest, and on earth *peace* among those with whom he is pleased!"

LUKE 2:13–14 ESV

I am *the Word that became flesh*. I have always been, and I will always be. *In the beginning was the Word, and the Word was with God, and the Word was God.* As you think about Me as a baby, born in Bethlehem, do not lose sight of My divinity. This baby who grew up and became a Man-Savior is also God Almighty! It could not have been otherwise. My sacrificial life and death would have been insufficient if I were not God. So rejoice that *the Word*, who entered the world as a helpless infant, is the same One who brought the world into existence.

Though I was rich, for your sake I became poor, so that you might become rich. No Christmas present could ever compare with the treasure you have in Me! I remove your sins *as far as the east is from the west*—freeing you from all condemnation. I gift you with unimaginably glorious Life that will never end! The best response to this astonishing Gift is to embrace it joyfully and gratefully.

In the beginning was the Word, and the Word was with God, and the Word was God. . . . The Word became flesh and made his dwelling among us. We have seen his glory, the glory of the One and Only, who came from the Father, full of grace and truth.

JOHN 1:1, 14

In the past God spoke to our forefathers through the prophets at many times and in various ways, but in these last days he has spoken to us by his Son, whom he appointed heir of all things, and through whom he made the universe.

HEBREWS 1:1–2

For you know the grace of our Lord Jesus Christ, that though He was rich, yet for your sake He became poor, so that you through His poverty might become rich.

2 CORINTHIANS 8:9 NASB

As far as the east is from the
west, so far has He *removed*
our *transgressions* from us.

PSALM 103:12 NKJV

I speak to you from the depths of eternity. *Before the world was formed, I AM!* You hear Me in the depths of your being, where I have taken up residence. *I am Christ in you, the hope of Glory.* I, your Lord and Savior, am alive within you. Learn to tune in to My living Presence by seeking Me in silence.

As you celebrate the wonder of My birth in Bethlehem, celebrate also your rebirth into eternal life. This everlasting gift was the sole purpose of My entering your sin-stained world. Receive My gift with awe and humility. Take time to explore the vast dimensions of My Love. Allow thankfulness to flow freely from your heart in response to My glorious gift. *Let My Peace rule in your heart, and be thankful.*

Before the mountains were brought forth or ever You
had formed and given birth to the earth and the world,
even from everlasting to everlasting You are God.

PSALM 90:2 AMP

To them God has chosen to make known among
the Gentiles the glorious riches of this mystery,
which is Christ in you, the hope of glory.

COLOSSIANS 1:27

In reply Jesus declared, "I tell you the truth, no one can
see the kingdom of God unless he is born again."

JOHN 3:3

Let the *peace* of Christ rule in your hearts, since as members of one body you were called to peace. And be *thankful*.

COLOSSIANS 3:15

I give you Joy that is independent of circumstances; I give you Myself! *All the treasures of wisdom and knowledge are hidden in Me.* Because I am infinitely wise and all-knowing, you will never run out of treasures to search for.

I am a wellspring of Joy—eager to overflow into your life. Open wide your heart, mind, and spirit to receive Me in full measure. My Joy is not of this world; it can coexist with the most difficult circumstances. No matter what is happening in your life, *the Light of My Presence* continues to shine upon you. Look up to Me with a trusting heart. If you persist in searching for Me, My Joy-Light can break through the darkest storm clouds. Let this heavenly Light soak into you, brightening your perspective and filling you with transcendent delight.

Remember that you have *an inheritance in heaven that can never perish, spoil, or fade*. Since *you believe in Me, inexpressible, glorious Joy* is yours—now and forever!

. . . In whom are hidden all the treasures
of wisdom and knowledge.

COLOSSIANS 2:3

Blessed are those who have learned to acclaim you, who
walk in the light of your presence, O LORD. They rejoice in
your name all day long; they exult in your righteousness.

PSALM 89:15—16

Praise be to the God and Father of our Lord Jesus
Christ! In his great mercy he has given us new birth
into a living hope through the resurrection of Jesus
Christ from the dead, and into an inheritance that can
never perish, spoil or fade—kept in heaven for you. . . .
Though you have not seen him, you love him; and even
though you do not see him now, you believe in him
and are filled with an inexpressible and glorious joy.

1 PETER 1:3—4, 8

*S*eeking to please Me is a joyous way to live. Of course, *without faith it is impossible to please Me.* You must really *believe that I exist and that I reward those who earnestly seek Me.*

Living to please Me is a wise investment—not only for rewards in heaven but also for daily pleasure on earth. I am meant to be the Center of your existence, the Sun around which you orbit. When you live this way—enjoying Me, serving Me, desiring to please Me—you stay in your proper orbit. When you live in a self-centered way, you go off course.

The challenge is to keep Me central in what you do, say, and think. This battle begins in your mind, so work on *taking captive every thought to make it obedient to Me.* Study My Word to find out what pleases Me, and remember how wonderfully well I love you. Awareness of My amazing Love will help you stay in orbit around the Son—enjoying the radiant pleasures of My Presence.

And without faith it is impossible to please God, because anyone who comes to him must believe that he exists and that he rewards those who earnestly seek him.

HEBREWS 11:6

We demolish arguments and every pretension that sets itself up against the knowledge of God, and we take captive every thought to make it obedient to Christ.

2 CORINTHIANS 10:5

We . . . do not cease to pray for you, and to ask . . . that you may walk worthy of the Lord, fully pleasing Him, being fruitful in every good work and increasing in the knowledge of God.

COLOSSIANS 1:9–10 NKJV

I am the gift that continuously gives—bounteously, with no strings attached. Unconditional Love is such a radical concept that even My most devoted followers fail to grasp it fully. Absolutely nothing in heaven or on earth can cause Me to stop loving you. You may *feel* more loved when you are performing according to your expectations. But My Love for you is perfect; therefore it is not subject to variation. What *does* vary is your awareness of My loving Presence.

When you are dissatisfied with your behavior, you tend to feel unworthy of My Love. You may unconsciously punish yourself by withdrawing from Me and attributing the distance between us to My displeasure. Instead of returning to Me and receiving My Love, you attempt to earn My approval by trying harder. All the while, I am aching to hold you in *My everlasting arms*, to enfold you in My Love. When you are feeling unworthy or unloved, come to Me. Then ask for receptivity to *My unfailing Love*.

If anyone acknowledges that Jesus is the Son of God, God lives in him and he in God. And so we know and rely on the love God has for us. God is love. Whoever lives in love lives in God, and God in him. . . . There is no fear in love. But perfect love drives out fear, because fear has to do with punishment. The one who fears is not made perfect in love.

1 JOHN 4:15–16, 18

The eternal God is your refuge, and underneath are the everlasting arms.

DEUTERONOMY 33:27

But I trust in your unfailing love; my heart rejoices in your salvation.

PSALM 13:5

I am Immanuel—*God with you*—and I am enough! When things in your life are flowing smoothly, it is easy to trust in My sufficiency. However, when you encounter rough patches—one after another after another—you may sometimes feel that My provision is inadequate. This is when your mind tends to go into high gear: obsessing about ways to make things better. There is nothing wrong with seeking solutions, but problem-solving can turn into an addiction: your mind spinning with so many plans and possibilities that you become confused and exhausted.

To protect yourself from this mental exhaustion, you need to remind yourself that *I am with you always*, taking care of you. It is possible to *rejoice in Me*—to proclaim My sufficiency—even during the most difficult times. This is a supernatural work, empowered by My Spirit who lives in you. It is also a decision that you make—day by day and moment by moment. Choose to *be joyful in Me, your Savior*, for I am indeed enough!

"She will bring forth a Son, and you shall call His name JESUS, for He will save His people from their sins." So all this was done that it might be fulfilled which was spoken by the Lord through the prophet, saying: "Behold, the virgin shall be with child, and bear a Son, and they shall call His name Immanuel," which is translated, "God with us."

MATTHEW 1:21–23 NKJV

"[Go and make disciples,] teaching them to obey everything I have commanded you. And surely I am with you always, to the very end of the age."

MATTHEW 28:20

Though the fig tree does not bud and there are no grapes on the vines, though the olive crop fails and the fields produce no food, though there are no sheep in the pen and no cattle in the stalls, yet I will rejoice in the LORD, I will be joyful in God my Savior.

HABAKKUK 3:17–18

I am leading you along a way that is uniquely right for you. The closer to Me you grow, the more fully you become your true self—the one I designed you to be. Because you are one of a kind, the path you are traveling with Me diverges increasingly from that of other people. However, in My mysterious wisdom and ways, I enable you to follow this solitary path while staying in close contact with others. In fact, the more completely you devote yourself to Me, the more freely you can love people.

Marvel at the beauty of a life intertwined with My Presence. Rejoice as we journey together in intimate communion. Enjoy the adventure of finding yourself through losing yourself in Me.

Therefore, if anyone is in Christ, he is a new creation; the old has gone, the new has come!

2 CORINTHIANS 5:17

For we are God's workmanship, created in Christ Jesus to do good works, which God prepared in advance for us to do.

EPHESIANS 2:10

Dear friends, let us love one another, for love comes from God. Everyone who loves has been born of God and knows God. Whoever does not love does not know God, because God is love.

1 JOHN 4:7–8

"Remain in me, and I will remain in you. No branch can bear *fruit* by itself; it must remain in the *vine*. Neither can you bear fruit unless you *remain* in me."

JOHN 15:4

Worship Me in the beauty of holiness. There is a great deal of beauty in your world, but none of it is perfectly holy. So *the beauty of holiness* is something you know only in part—for now. Someday *you will know fully, even as you are fully known.* Even now, though, awareness of My holiness stimulates worship. Pondering My perfection—untainted by even a speck of sin—delights you and fills you with awe. I invite you to join with the angels in proclaiming: *"Holy, holy, holy is the Lord of hosts; the whole earth is full of His Glory!"*

Worshiping Me well transforms you—changing you more and more into the one I designed you to be. Genuine worship requires that you know Me as I truly am. You cannot comprehend Me perfectly or completely, but you *can* strive to know Me accurately, as I am revealed in the Bible. By deepening your understanding of Me, you are transformed and I am glorified—in beautiful worship.

Give unto the Lᴏʀᴅ the glory due to His name;
worship the Lᴏʀᴅ in the beauty of holiness.

Psalm 29:2 nkjv

⁓

Now we see but a poor reflection as in a mirror;
then we shall see face to face. Now I know in part;
then I shall know fully, even as I am fully known.

1 Corinthians 13:12

⁓

One [seraphim] cried to another and said: "Holy, holy, holy
is the Lᴏʀᴅ of hosts; the whole earth is full of His glory!"

Isaiah 6:3 nkjv

et Me fill you with My Joy and Peace. They flow into you as you sit quietly in My Presence, trusting Me in the depths of your being. These blessings are essential for nourishing your soul. *The Joy of the Lord is your strength*, so don't neglect this delightful gift. It is for all times and all circumstances, though sometimes you have to search for it. You also need My Peace at all times, and I bestow it on you freely as you trust in Me.

Remember that I am *the God of hope*. The hope I offer is not wishful thinking. It is absolutely certain, even though it refers to things not yet fully realized. It is utterly secure because I Myself obtained it through My finished work on the cross. This hope is the foundation of the Joy and Peace you find in Me. No matter how hard your life may be at this time, you have full assurance that endless delight awaits you in heaven, where I have *prepared a place for you*. As you ponder this glorious truth, you can enjoy hope that *overflows by the Power of the Holy Spirit*.

May the God of hope fill you with all joy and peace
as you trust in him, so that you may overflow
with hope by the power of the Holy Spirit.

ROMANS 15:13

Then [Nehemiah] said to [all the people of Israel],
"Go your way, eat the fat, drink the sweet, and send
portions to those for whom nothing is prepared;
for this day is holy to our Lord. Do not sorrow,
for the joy of the LORD is your strength."

NEHEMIAH 8:10 NKJV

"In My Father's house are many mansions; if it
were not so, I would have told you. I go to prepare
a place for you. And if I go and prepare a place for
you, I will come again and receive you to Myself;
that where I am, there you may be also."

JOHN 14:2–3 NKJV

I am a God of both intricate detail and overflowing abundance. When you entrust the details of your life to Me, you are surprised by how thoroughly I answer your petitions. I take pleasure in hearing your prayers, so feel free to bring Me all your requests. The more you pray, the more answers you can receive. Best of all, your faith is strengthened as you see how precisely I respond to your specific prayers.

Because I am infinite in all My ways, you need not fear that I will run out of resources. *Abundance* is at the very heart of who I am. Come to Me in joyful expectation of receiving all you need—and sometimes much more! I delight in showering blessings on My beloved children. Come to Me with open hands and heart, ready to receive all I have for you.

How priceless is your unfailing love! Both high and low among men find refuge in the shadow of your wings. They feast on the abundance of your house; you give them drink from your river of delights. For with you is the fountain of life; in your light we see light.

PSALM 36:7—9

"I will bless her with abundant provisions;
her poor will I satisfy with food."

PSALM 132:15

When they had all had enough to eat, he said to his disciples, "Gather the pieces that are left over. Let nothing be wasted." So they gathered them and filled twelve baskets with the pieces of the five barley loaves left over by those who had eaten.

JOHN 6:12—13

*Y*ou are Mine for all time—and beyond time, into eternity. No power can deny you your inheritance in heaven. I want you to realize how utterly secure you are! Even if you falter as you journey through life, I will never let go of your hand.

Knowing that your future is absolutely assured can free you to live abundantly today. I have prepared this day for you with the most tender concern and attention to detail. Instead of approaching the day as a blank page that you need to fill up, try living it in a responsive mode, being on the lookout for all that I am doing. This sounds easy, but it requires a deep level of trust, based on the knowledge that *My way is perfect.*

Praise be to the God and Father of our Lord Jesus Christ! In his great mercy he has given us new birth into a living hope through the resurrection of Jesus Christ from the dead, and into an inheritance that can never perish, spoil or fade—kept in heaven for you.

1 Peter 1:3—4

If the Lord delights in a man's way, he makes his steps firm; though he stumble, he will not fall, for the Lord upholds him with his hand.

Psalm 37:23—24

As for God, his way is perfect; the word of the Lord is flawless. He is a shield for all who take refuge in him.

Psalm 18:30

*R*emember Me on your bed; think of Me through the *watches of the night.* When you are wakeful during the night, thoughts can fly at you from all directions. Unless you take charge of them, you are likely to become anxious. Your best strategy is to think about Me during your night watches. Start communicating with Me about whatever is on your mind. *Cast all your anxiety on Me because I care for you.* I am taking care of you! This makes it possible for you to relax and *rejoice in the shadow of My wings.*

When you remember Me during the night, think about who I really am. Ponder My perfections: My Love, Joy, and Peace. Rejoice in My majesty, wisdom, grace, and mercy. Find comfort in My names: Shepherd, Savior, Immanuel, Prince of Peace. Be awed by My Power and Glory, for I am King of kings and Lord of lords. Thus you worship Me and enjoy My Presence. These thoughts of Me will clear your mind— helping you see things from My perspective—and refresh your entire being.

On my bed I remember you;
I think of you through the
watches of the *night*.

Cast all your anxiety on [God] because he cares for you.

1 PETER 5:7

Because You have been my help, therefore in
the shadow of Your wings I will rejoice.

PSALM 63:7 NKJV

Fight the good fight of the faith. Take hold of the eternal
life to which you were called. . . . I charge you to keep
this command without spot or blame until the appearing
of our Lord Jesus Christ, which God will bring about in
his own time—God, the blessed and only Ruler, the King
of kings and Lord of lords, who alone is immortal and
who lives in unapproachable light, whom no one has
seen or can see. To him be honor and might forever.

1 TIMOTHY 6:12—16

Hold My hand, and walk joyously with Me through this day. Together we will savor the pleasures and endure the difficulties it brings. Be on the lookout for everything I have prepared for you: stunning scenery, bracing winds of adventure, cozy nooks for resting when you are weary, and much more. I am your Guide, as well as your constant Companion. I know every step of the journey ahead of you, all the way to heaven.

You don't have to choose between staying close to Me and staying on course. Since *I am the Way*, staying close to Me is staying on course. As you focus your thoughts on Me, I will guide you carefully along today's journey. Don't worry about what is around the next bend. Just concentrate on enjoying My Presence and staying in step with Me.

I can do all things through Christ who strengthens me.

PHILIPPIANS 4:13 NKJV

The LORD will guide you always; he will satisfy your
needs in a sun-scorched land and will strengthen
your frame. You will be like a well-watered
garden, like a spring whose waters never fail.

ISAIAH 58:11

Jesus answered, "I am the way and the truth and the
life. No one comes to the Father except through me."

JOHN 14:6

Devote yourselves to *prayer*,
being *watchful* and thankful.

COLOSSIANS 4:2

Even though you do not see Me, you believe in Me. I am far more real—complete, unchanging, unlimited—than the things you can see. When you believe in Me, you are trusting in rock-solid Reality. I am the indestructible *Rock* on which you can keep standing, no matter what your circumstances may be. And because you belong to Me, I am devoted to you. Beloved, I encourage you to *take refuge in Me.*

Believing in Me has innumerable benefits. The most precious one is *the salvation of your soul*—forever and ever. Your belief in Me also enhances your present life immensely, making it possible for you to know who you are and Whose you are. As you stay in communication with Me, I help you find your way through this fallen world with hope in your heart. All of this enlarges your capacity for Joy. The more you seek Me and the more fully you know Me, the more I can fill you with *inexpressible and glorious Joy*!

Though you have not seen him, you love him;
and even though you do not see him now, you
believe in him and are filled with an inexpressible
and glorious joy, for you are receiving the goal
of your faith, the salvation of your souls.

1 PETER 1:8–9

The LORD is my rock, my fortress and my deliverer;
my God is my rock, in whom I take refuge. He is my
shield and the horn of my salvation, my stronghold.

PSALM 18:2

But if we hope for what we do not see, we
eagerly wait for it with perseverance.

ROMANS 8:25 NKJV

*D*raw near to Me with a thankful heart, aware that your cup is overflowing with blessings. Gratitude enables you to perceive Me more clearly and to rejoice in our Love-relationship. *Nothing can separate you from My loving Presence!* That is the basis of your security. Whenever you start to feel anxious, remind yourself that your security rests in Me alone, and I am totally trustworthy.

You will never be in control of your life circumstances, but you can relax and trust in My control. Instead of striving for a predictable, safe lifestyle, seek to know Me in greater depth and breadth. I long to make your life a glorious adventure, but you must stop clinging to old ways. I am always doing something new within My beloved ones. Be on the lookout for all that I have prepared for you.

For I am convinced that neither death nor life, neither
angels nor demons, neither the present nor the future,
nor any powers, neither height nor depth, nor anything
else in all creation, will be able to separate us from
the love of God that is in Christ Jesus our Lord.

ROMANS 8:38−39

When I am afraid, I will trust in you. In God,
whose word I praise, in God I trust; I will not
be afraid. What can mortal man do to me?

PSALM 56:3−4

"See, I am doing a new thing! Now it springs up;
do you not perceive it? I am making a way in
the desert and streams in the wasteland."

ISAIAH 43:19

*T*hank Me throughout this day for My Presence and My Peace. These are gifts of supernatural proportions. Ever since the resurrection, I have comforted My followers with these messages: *Peace be with you*, and *I am with you always*. Listen as I offer you My Peace and Presence in full measure. The best way to receive these glorious gifts is to thank Me for them.

It is impossible to spend too much time thanking and praising Me. I created you first and foremost to glorify Me. Thanksgiving and praise put you in proper relationship with Me, opening the way for My riches to flow into you. As you thank Me for My Presence and Peace, you appropriate My richest gifts.

While they were still talking about this, Jesus himself stood among them and said to them, "Peace be with you."

LUKE 24:36

"And teaching them to obey everything I have commanded you. And surely I am with you always, to the very end of the age."

MATTHEW 28:20

Through Jesus, therefore, let us continually offer to God a sacrifice of praise—the fruit of lips that confess his name.

HEBREWS 13:15

Thanks be to *God* for
His *indescribable* gift!

2 CORINTHIANS 9:15 NKJV

I want you to learn to *be joyful always* by connecting your Joy to Me first and foremost. One way of doing this is to remember that I love you at all times and in all circumstances. *Though the mountains be shaken and the hills be removed, My unfailing Love for you will* not *be shaken.* So don't give in to the temptation to doubt My Love when things don't go as you would like or when you have failed in some way. My loving Presence is the solid rock on which you can always stand— knowing that in Me you are eternally secure. I am *the Lord who has compassion on you*!

Another way of increasing your Joy is to *give thanks in all circumstances.* Ask My Spirit to help you view your life through the lens of gratitude. Search for blessings scattered along your pathway—even during your hardest times—and thank Me for each one. I encourage you to look steadily through your lens of gratefulness by *thinking about things that are excellent and worthy of praise.*

Be joyful always; pray continually; give
thanks in all circumstances, for this is
God's will for you in Christ Jesus.

1 Thessalonians 5:16–18

"Though the mountains be shaken and the hills
be removed, yet my unfailing love for you will not
be shaken nor my covenant of peace be removed,"
says the Lord, who has compassion on you.

Isaiah 54:10

And now, dear brothers and sisters, one final thing.
Fix your thoughts on what is true, and honorable,
and right, and pure, and lovely, and admirable. Think
about things that are excellent and worthy of praise.

Philippians 4:8 NLT

I am the Lord of Peace. I give you Peace at all times and in every way. There is a deep, gaping hole within you that can be filled only by My peaceful Presence. People who don't know Me try to fill that emptiness in many different ways, or they simply pretend it isn't there. Even My children often fail to recognize the full extent of their need: *at all times* and in every situation. But recognizing your neediness is only half the battle. The other half is to believe I can—and will—supply all you need.

Shortly before My death, I promised Peace to My disciples—and to all who would become My followers. I made it clear that this is a gift: something I provide freely and lovingly. So your responsibility is to *receive* this glorious gift, acknowledging to Me not only your need but also your desire. Then wait expectantly in My Presence, ready to receive My Peace in full measure. If you like, you can express your openness by saying, "Jesus, I receive Your Peace."

Now may the Lord of peace himself give you peace at all times and in every way. The Lord be with all of you.

2 THESSALONIANS 3:16

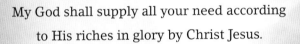

My God shall supply all your need according to His riches in glory by Christ Jesus.

PHILIPPIANS 4:19 NKJV

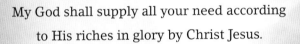

"Peace I leave with you; my peace I give you. I do not give to you as the world gives. Do not let your hearts be troubled and do not be afraid."

JOHN 14:27

I am with you, watching over you constantly. I am Immanuel (*God with you*); My Presence enfolds you in radiant Love. Nothing, including the brightest blessings and the darkest trials, can separate you from Me. Some of My children find Me more readily during dark times, when difficulties force them to depend on Me. Others feel closer to Me when their lives are filled with good things. They respond with thanksgiving and praise, thus opening wide the door to My Presence.

I know precisely what you need to draw nearer to Me. Go through each day looking for what I have prepared for you. Accept every event as My hand-tailored provision for your needs. When you view your life this way, the most reasonable response is to be thankful. Do not reject any of My gifts; find Me in every situation.

"The virgin will be with child and will give birth to a son, and they will call him Immanuel"—which means, "God with us."

MATTHEW 1:23

Those who look to him are radiant; their faces are never covered with shame.

PSALM 34:5

So then, just as you received Christ Jesus as Lord, continue to live in him, rooted and built up in him, strengthened in the faith as you were taught, and overflowing with thankfulness.

COLOSSIANS 2:6–7

No matter how lonely you may feel, you are never alone. Christmas can be a hard time for people who are separated from loved ones. The separation may be a result of death, divorce, distance, or other causes. The holiday merriment around you can intensify your sense of aloneness. But all My children have a resource that is more than adequate to help them: My continual Presence.

Remember this prophecy about Me: *"The virgin . . . will give birth to a Son, and they will call Him Immanuel"—which means "God with us."* Long before I was born, I was proclaimed to be the God who is *with you.* This is rock-solid truth that nobody and no circumstance can take away from you.

Whenever you're feeling lonely, take time to enjoy My Presence. Thank Me for *wrapping you with a robe of righteousness* to make you righteous. Ask Me—*the God of hope*—to *fill you with Joy and Peace.* Then, through the help of My Spirit, you can *overflow with hope* into the lives of other people.

"The virgin will be with child and will
give birth to a son, and they will call him
Immanuel"—which means, "God with us."

MATTHEW 1:23

I will rejoice greatly in the LORD, my soul will exult
in my God; for He has clothed me with garments
of salvation, He has wrapped me with a robe of
righteousness, as a bridegroom decks himself with a
garland, and as a bride adorns herself with her jewels.

ISAIAH 61:10 NASB

For He made Him who knew no sin to be sin for us, that
we might become the righteousness of God in Him.

2 CORINTHIANS 5:21 NKJV

May the God of *hope* fill you with all *joy* and *peace* as you *trust* in him, so that you may overflow with hope by the *power* of the Holy Spirit.

ROMANS 15:13

I, your Savior, am *Mighty God!* Much of the focus during Advent is on the Baby in the manger. I did indeed begin My life on earth in this humble way. I set aside My Glory and took on human flesh. But I continued to be God—able to live a perfect, sinless life and perform mighty miracles. *I, your God, am with you—mighty to save!* Be blessed by this combination of My tender nearness and My majestic Power.

When I entered the world, *I came to that which was My own,* because everything was made through Me. *But My own did not receive Me. Yet to all who received Me, to those who believed in My Name, I gave the right to become children of God.* This gift of salvation is of infinite value. It gives meaning and direction to your life—and makes heaven your final destination. During this season of giving and receiving presents, remember that the ultimate present is eternal Life. Respond to this glorious gift by *rejoicing in Me always!*

For unto us a Child is born, unto us a Son is given;
and the government will be upon His shoulder.
And His name will be called Wonderful, Counselor,
Mighty God, Everlasting Father, Prince of Peace.

ISAIAH 9:6 NKJV

"The LORD your God is with you, he is mighty to save.
He will take great delight in you, he will quiet you
with his love, he will rejoice over you with singing."

ZEPHANIAH 3:17

He came to that which was his own, but his
own did not receive him. Yet to all who received
him, to those who believed in his name, he
gave the right to become children of God.

JOHN 1:11–12

Rejoice in
the *Lord* always.
I will say it
again: Rejoice!

PHILIPPIANS 4:4

I *have done great things for you*, so let Me fill you with Joy. Take ample time to ponder all I have done for you. Rejoice in My goodness and My greatness as you remember My marvelous deeds. Rest in My intimate Presence; relax in My *everlasting arms*. I long to fill you with Joy, but you must collaborate with Me in this process.

Do not be like a spoiled child on Christmas Day—hastily tearing open all the presents and then saying, "Is that all?" Every single day is a precious gift from Me! *Search for Me* within the boundaries of this day, and you will surely find Me. I am present not only in pleasant things but also in unwanted circumstances. My Joy is sufficient for all situations, and I adjust it according to your need. When things are going your way, My gladness intensifies your delight. When you encounter hard things, I give you a deep, bold Joy that clings to Me for help. Receiving My Joy requires not only time but also courage.

The LORD has done great things for
us, and we are filled with joy.

PSALM 126:3

The eternal God is your refuge, and
underneath are the everlasting arms.

DEUTERONOMY 33:27 NKJV

"You will seek Me and find Me, when you
search for Me with all your heart."

JEREMIAH 29:13 NKJV

In this you greatly *rejoice*, though
now for a little while you may have
had to suffer grief in all kinds of
trials. These have come so that your
faith—of greater worth than gold,
which perishes even though refined by
fire—may be proved *genuine* and may
result in praise, glory and honor when
Jesus Christ is revealed. Though you
have not seen him, you love him; and
even though you do not see him now,
you *believe* in him and are filled with
an inexpressible and *glorious* joy.

1 PETER 1:6—8

Let My Peace rule in your heart, and be thankful. And let My Spirit help you in this challenging endeavor. The Spirit lives in you, so His fruit—*Love, Joy, Peace*—is always accessible to you. A simple way to request His help is to pray: "Holy Spirit, fill me with Your Peace." Try sitting in a quiet place until you feel relaxed and calm. When you are thoroughly relaxed, it is easier to seek My Face and enjoy My Presence.

While you rest in My Presence, take time to thank Me for the many good things I give you. As you focus on Me and My bountiful blessings, let your heart swell with gratitude and even *leap for Joy*. One of the most precious gifts imaginable is My *robe of righteousness*—to cover your sins. This glorious *garment of salvation* is a priceless blessing for all who trust Me as Savior. The gift of eternal righteousness, purchased through My blood, provides a firm foundation for both Peace and Joy.

Let the peace of Christ rule in your hearts,
since as members of one body you were
called to peace. And be thankful.

COLOSSIANS 3:15

But the fruit of the Spirit is love, joy, peace,
longsuffering, kindness, goodness, faithfulness,
gentleness, self-control. Against such there is no law.

GALATIANS 5:22–23 NKJV

The LORD is my strength and my shield; my heart
trusts in him, and I am helped. My heart leaps
for joy and I will give thanks to him in song.

PSALM 28:7

I *delight* greatly in the LORD;
my soul rejoices in my *God*.
For he has clothed me with
garments of salvation and arrayed
me in a robe of *righteousness*,
as a bridegroom adorns his
head like a priest, and as a bride
adorns herself with her *jewels*.

ISAIAH 61:10

I am preparing you for what is on the road ahead, just around the bend. Take time to be still in My Presence so that I can strengthen you. The busier you become, the more you need this time apart with Me. So many people think that time spent with Me is a luxury they cannot afford. As a result, they live and work in their own strength—until that becomes depleted. Then they either cry out to Me for help or turn away in bitterness.

How much better it is to walk close to Me, depending on My strength and trusting Me in every situation. If you live in this way, you will *do* less but *accomplish* far more. Your unhurried pace of living will stand out in this rush-crazed age. Some people may deem you lazy, but many more will be blessed by your peacefulness. Walk in the Light with Me, and you will reflect Me to the watching world.

Since ancient times no one has heard, no ear has perceived, no eye has seen any God besides you, who acts on behalf of those who wait for him.

ISAIAH 64:4

"I am the vine; you are the branches. If a man remains in me and I in him, he will bear much fruit; apart from me you can do nothing."

JOHN 15:5

For with you is the fountain of life; in your light we see light.

PSALM 36:9

*R*elax, My child. I'm in control. Let these words wash over you repeatedly, like soothing waves on a beautiful beach, assuring you of My endless Love. You waste a lot of time and energy trying to figure out things before their time has come. Meanwhile, I am working to prepare the way before you. So be on the lookout for some wonderful surprises— circumstances that only *I* could have orchestrated.

Remember that you are My beloved. I am on your side, and I want what is best for you. Someone who is loved by a generous, powerful person can expect to receive an abundance of blessings. *You* are loved by the King of the universe, and I have good plans for you. As you look ahead into the unknown future, relax in the knowledge of who you are—*the one I love*. Cling to My hand, and go forward with confidence. While you and I walk together along *the path of Life*, your trust in Me will fill your heart with Joy and your mind with Peace.

"For I know the plans I have for you," declares the Lord, "plans to prosper you and not to harm you, plans to give you hope and a future."

JEREMIAH 29:11

About Benjamin he said: "Let the beloved of the Lord rest secure in him, for he shields him all day long, and the one the Lord loves rests between his shoulders."

DEUTERONOMY 33:12

You will show me the path of life; in Your presence is fullness of joy; at Your right hand are pleasures forevermore.

PSALM 16:11 NKJV

*D*on't be afraid to be happy. Because you are Mine, you can expect to experience some happiness—even in this broken world. Yet anxiety sometimes intrudes upon your carefree moments. You start wondering if there are things you should be doing or plans you should be making. Your underlying feeling is that it isn't safe to let down your guard and simply be happy in the moment. How wrong this is, My child!

I have called you to *cease striving*—let go, relax—*and know that I am God.* You may think that you need to have all your ducks in a row before you can relax and enjoy My Presence. But consider the overall context of this command: *though the earth give way and the mountains fall into the heart of the sea.* The psalmist who penned these words was describing a terrifying catastrophe. So you don't need to wait till you've solved all the problems in your life; this very moment is the right time to enjoy Me. Come boldly into My Presence, saying, "Jesus, I choose to enjoy You—here and now."

Happy are the people whose God is the LORD!

PSALM 144:15 NKJV

Cease striving and know that I am God; I will be exalted
among the nations, I will be exalted in the earth.

PSALM 46:10 NASB

God is our refuge and strength, an ever-present
help in trouble. Therefore we will not fear, though
the earth give way and the mountains fall into the
heart of the sea, though its waters roar and foam
and the mountains quake with their surging.

PSALM 46:1–3

o not hesitate to receive Joy from Me, for I bestow it on you abundantly. The more you rest in My Presence, the more freely My blessings flow into you. In the Light of My Love, you are gradually *transformed from glory to glory*. It is through spending time with Me that you realize *how wide and long and high and deep is My Love for you.*

Sometimes the relationship I offer you seems too good to be true. I pour My very Life into you, and all you have to do is receive Me. In a world characterized by working and taking, the admonition to rest and receive seems too easy. There is a close connection between receiving and believing: As you trust Me more and more, you are able to receive Me and My blessings abundantly. *Be still, and know that I am God.*

But we all, with unveiled face, beholding as
in a mirror the glory of the Lord, are being
transformed into the same image from glory
to glory, just as from the Lord, the Spirit.

2 CORINTHIANS 3:18 NASB

So that Christ may dwell in your hearts through faith.
And I pray that you, being rooted and established in love,
may have power, together with all the saints, to grasp how
wide and long and high and deep is the love of Christ,
and to know this love that surpasses knowledge—that you
may be filled to the measure of all the fullness of God.

EPHESIANS 3:17–19

"Be *still*, and know that I am God; I will be *exalted* among the nations, I will be exalted in the *earth*."

PSALM 46:10

*A*s this year draws to a close, receive My Peace. This is still your deepest need, and I, your *Prince of Peace*, long to pour Myself into your neediness. My abundance and your emptiness are a perfect match. I designed you to have no sufficiency of your own. I created you as a *jar of clay*, set apart for sacred use. I want you to be filled with My very Being, permeated through and through with Peace.

Thank Me for My peaceful Presence, regardless of your feelings. Whisper My Name in loving tenderness. *My Peace*, which lives continually in your spirit, will gradually work its way through your entire being.

For to us a child is born, to us a son is given, and
the government will be on his shoulders. And
he will be called Wonderful Counselor, Mighty
God, Everlasting Father, Prince of Peace.

ISAIAH 9:6

But we have this treasure in jars of clay to show that
this all-surpassing power is from God and not from us.

2 CORINTHIANS 4:7

"But the Counselor, the Holy Spirit, whom the Father will
send in my name, will teach you all things and will remind
you of everything I have said to you. Peace I leave with you;
my peace I give you. I do not give to you as the world gives.
Do not let your hearts be troubled and do not be afraid."

JOHN 14:26–27

As you come to the end of this year, take some time to look back—and also to look ahead. Ask Me to help you review the highlights of this year: hard times as well as good times. Try to see *Me* in these memories, for I have been close beside you—every step of the way.

When you were clinging to Me for help in the midst of tough times, I comforted you with My loving Presence. I was also richly present in circumstances that filled you with great Joy. I was with you on the mountain peaks, in the valleys, and everywhere in between.

Your future stretches out before you all the way into eternity. I am the Companion who will never leave you, the Guide who knows every step of the way ahead. The Joy that awaits you in paradise is *inexpressible and full of Glory*! As you prepare to step into a new year, let heaven's Light shine upon you and brighten the path just before you.

"For I am the LORD, your God, who takes hold of your right hand and says to you, Do not fear; I will help you."

ISAIAH 41:13

You will show me the path of life; in Your presence is fullness of joy; at Your right hand are pleasures forevermore.

PSALM 16:11 NKJV

For this God is our God for ever and ever; he will be our guide even to the end.

PSALM 48:14

Though you have not seen Him, you *love* Him, and though you do not see Him now, but *believe* in Him, you greatly *rejoice* with joy inexpressible and full of glory, obtaining as the outcome of your faith the *salvation* of your souls.

1 Peter 1:8–9 NASB

*D*o not dwell on the past. See, I am doing a new thing! As you begin a fresh year, rejoice that I am continually working newness into your life. Don't let recent disappointments and failures define you or dampen your expectations. This is the time to make a fresh start! I am a God of unlimited creativity; expect Me to do surprising things in this year that stretches out before you.

Today is a precious gift. The present moment is where I meet with you, beloved. So seek My Face throughout *this day that I have made*. I have carefully prepared it for you—with tender attention to every detail. I want you to *rejoice and be glad in it*.

Search for signs of My loving Presence as you journey along *the path of Life*. Look for the little pleasures I have strewn alongside your pathway—sometimes in surprising places—and thank Me for each one. Your thankfulness will keep you close to Me and help you find Joy in your journey.

"Forget the former things; do not dwell on the past. See, I am doing a new thing! Now it springs up; do you not perceive it? I am making a way in the desert and streams in the wasteland."

ISAIAH 43:18—19

❧

This is the day that the LORD has made; let us rejoice and be glad in it.

PSALM 118:24 ESV

You will show me the *path* of
life; in Your *presence* is fullness
of *joy*; at Your right hand are
pleasures *forevermore*.

Psalm 16:11 NKJV